BLOGGING SECRETS REVIEWED

The Beginners' Guide on How to Make Money Online Blogging

GODWINS INLINE

BLOGGING SECRETS REVIEWED

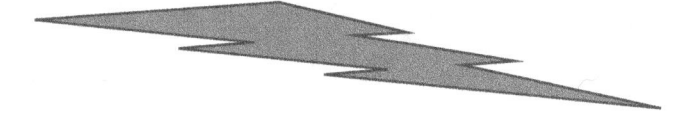

Dedicated to every online entrepreneur who're

just starting out.

Copyright

No part of this book is allowed to be reproduced in any form without approval from the author.

Other books by the author:

The $3,000 Blueprint

Online Passive Income

Table of Content

CHAPTER 1

Getting Started with Online Blogging

Deciding On a Niche and Blog Topic

Choosing the right niche and blog topic is one of the most critical decisions when launching a new blog. With over 600 million blogs on the internet, standing out and attracting an audience requires zeroing in on a specific, well-defined niche and topic that you're deeply passionate about.

Rather than simply blogging about "health" or "fitness," identify a narrow segment that clearly states what makes your content unique. For example, "Intermittent Fasting Tips for Women Over 40" or "Marathon Training Meal Plans for Vegetarians". Think deeply about your own expertise, interests, and background to determine a niche that you can bring unique authority or a fresh perspective to.

Conduct detailed niche research before deciding by brainstorming list of potential blog ideas and using online tools to assess factors like search volume, competition levels in Google, ease of monetization, and more. Resources like Google's Keyword Planner, SEMRush, and Ubersuggest can provide data-driven insights into which niches have enough interest and search traffic versus being too competitive.

Aim for niches with at least 1,000-10,000 monthly searches, moderate competition scores, and interesting "long tail" keyword opportunities you can target in your content. Track down forums and groups related to your shortlisted niches to better understand your target audiences pain points and burning questions. The best niches directly address clearly defined needs and problems for a specific subset of people.

While niche research is crucial, also self-reflect on your intrinsic motivations for blogging long-term. The niche that connects to your natural passions, background, skills, networks or life experiences tends to lead to more authentic, high quality content. For example, an ex-gymnast may choose the niche of "At Home Gymnastic Workouts" given her in-depth knowledge.

Moreover, narrow niches that tightly focus on specific "sub-passions" often build the strongest, most engaged communities around shared interests. A guitar lessons blog has wide appeal, but niche sites for "Blues Guitar Improvisation" or "Fingerstyle Classical Guitar" foster deeper connections and loyalty among more devoted enthusiasts.

Finally, examine your niche ideas through an entrepreneurial lens by determining monetization feasibility. Online income streams like affiliates, advertising, digital products and more require niches where people are actively spending money on solutions. Prioritize underserved, high-demand niches where you can solve pressing needs if income goals are a priority behind your blogging.

Meticulously researching niches, understanding your audience, playing to your strengths, and evaluating monetization potential are all key to landing on a winning niche and blog topic. Take time selecting a focused, profitable niche aligned to your passions and expertise - this foundations sets you up for growth, impact and income.

Creating a blog name and theme

Your blog's name and visual theme are pivotal first impressions that shape reader perceptions and signal what your blog stands for. Rather than rushing into generic names like "John's Blog," brainstorm strategic names that communicate your niche, hook reader curiosity and feel memorable. Meanwhile, your theme visuals should align to your niche and content style visually.

Assess the purpose behind your blog when naming. Are you blogging as an individual, business or organization? Does your focus lean more towards profession content, sharing a hobby, helping a community or entertaining through storytelling? All these nuances inform naming conventions. Personal name blogs take straightforward approaches like "Jane Smith Lifestyle Blog" while niche hobby sites may use humor, wordplay and domain hacks, like "Growth.Digital" or "BudgetEats.co".

To start brainstorming, mind map words and phrases related to your niche, ideal reader and topics using concept association techniques. Are certain key descriptors central to your content area? Do you want locality references if serving a regional audience or specific group like "AustinOver50"? What feeling-evoking adjectives match your tone like "Honest" or "Authentic" for transparent writing?

Assemble long lists of keyword-rich and feeling-conveying options at first, giving yourself flexibility. Check URL availability to verify domain possession viability early as well. While .COM sites are most prestigious, consider alternatives like .NET if your preferred .COM site is taken. Just steer clear of overused phrases in naming like "awesome" or "INSANE!" that feel forcefully salesy.

Now filter your lists by favorites that distinctly capture your niche and intended writing style or stand out memorably. Say them out loud, ask trusted contacts their preferences through a survey, cross-check business naming databases and thesaurus tools to catch issues. Avoid confusion with too general names that could describe thousands of existing sites. Add your name, location or niche signifiers that lend uniqueness.

From your refined possibilities, decide if separating your blog name from domain is advantageous. While using your brand name domain like PaulsCookingBlog.com is perfectly fine, sometimes SLDs like CookingWithPaul.com improve clickability. Avoid long blog names with excess words though, as concise, punchy names boost recall.

With your name selected, shift focus to visually representing your niche through your theme design and logo. Whether going fully DIY or using a tailored WordPress template, ensure visual cohesion across fonts, color scheme, layout, graphic choices and more that harmoniously state your focus.

For example, an edgy streetstyle blog may use graffiti style visual motifs, bold neon pop colors, urban photography and groovy display fonts. On the flip side, an antique furniture site channels classy muted tones, serif body text, ornate vintage graphics and polished gallery layouts.

Consider creating custom visual assets like your logo by using graphic design marketplaces like Fiverr and Upwork. Contract graphic designers, providing example themes with aesthetics you like and any name/icon ideas so they can represent your brand accordingly through images, color schemes and fonts that visitors instantly associate with your niche as soon as landing.

Thoughtfully naming and designing the visual skin of your blog crafts impactful first impressions visitors remember, so define the imagery, identity and initial feel that pulls your audience in. Through strategic titling choices and aligned, niche-appropriate themes, craft consistent branding around your distinct subject material and content mission that readers connect with.

Choosing a blogging platform

With dozens of blogging platforms available, from WordPress to Ghost to Medium, choosing the right software to host your blog requires evaluating multiple factors from ease of use to capabilities to cost. Approach platform selection as a pivotal long-term move - changing later may mean losing traffic or breaking reader routines.

Start by determining must-have features aligned to your skill level like simplicity for beginners versus programming customization for technical experts. Consider possibilities for integrating elements like multimedia, custom designs, an online store and email list development. Think through your growth vision for annual visitors, revenue streams from ads or products, and contributor team expansion needs too.

Weigh the reliability, speed and uptime track record for each platform along with security protections as well. While occasional outages hit even the most robust platforms, minimize risk by selecting well-funded established players with strong infrastructure reputations like WordPress.org or Squarespace.

From foundational hosting and functionality factors, assess options for technical ownership levels too. Self-hosted open source platforms like WordPress.org run on your own web hosting, offering full control over software customization at the cost of manual updates and security maintenance. These reward technical competence but require more responsibility than managed blog platforms.

Managed blogging platforms like WordPress.com or Wix handle hosting infrastructure, software updates, backups and security on your behalf while restricting plug-ins and design flexibility. Evaluate the available theme templates, ports, layout possibilities and ease of use if going this simpler route.

Pricing often dictates choices too. Managed WordPress plans start around $5-10 monthly for basic needs while robust self-hosted installs have minimums around $100 annually for hosting, themes, plugins and domain registration. Premium add-ons like email services, customized designs and ecommerce stores should be budgeted additionally in the hundreds per year as well depending on scale.

Alternatively, many bloggers start on free platforms like WordPress.com, Blogger or Medium without their own domain. While possible to upgrade later, initial platform switching once an audience is established brings significant traffic loss risk. Using personal domain emails and sites signals long-term professional dedication too compared to third-party.io sites.

For monetization needs like ad placements and affiliate programs, some platforms facilitate money-making far better too.

Evaluate the technology integrations available, community advice levels and platform incentives when income-generating. Optimization features for SEO and reader engagement should rank high for visibility help as well.

In balancing all key elements from usability to monetization potential and branding control, WordPress emerges as the dominant choice for over 60% of sites for good reason. Its open source CMS foundations enable robust expansion while simplified managed hosting through WordPress.com or specialty blog hosts like Bluehost cater to non-technical users with pre-configured installs. For easiest growth from hobby or professional blog to digital media empire, WordPress flexibility can't be beat.

Carefully weigh personal priorities from available time for site maintenance to long-term style possibilities against options like Ghost, Squarespace, Wix and more though. There's no universally "best" platform outside individual needs. Through listing must-have features however and trying free trials of a few frontrunners, the right blogging technology for you will become clear over time.

Setting Up Your Blog and Domain

With a clear content focus chosen, publishing platform selected, and basic web literacy, you're ready to start officially building your blog by registering a custom domain name and configuring the back-end settings. Treat your domain selection thoughtfully - it establishes your brand identity for readers. Meanwhile, properly personalizing key site settings gears your blog for growth through stronger visibility, user experience and content functionality.

Start by brainstorming a short, memorable domain name aligning to your niche using naming tips like keywords, name segments, and niche-relevant hooks related to your focus area. Verify availability through domain registrars like GoDaddy or Google Domains and register your top choice for roughly $12-15 annually.

For blogs seeking income streams, invest in the .com version of your domain when possible for prestige, trust and recall value among visitors. Once purchased, access your domain manager through your registrar to configure the name servers to your hosting provider if going the self-hosted route. This bridges your custom URL with the servers actually hosting your site files for seamless connectivity.

With your domain registered, begin installing and configuring your CMS platform like WordPress using their setup guides. For self-hosted users, first initialize WordPress installation through your hosting provider like Bluehost before customizing within your WordPress dashboard. For simpler managed

WordPress platforms, they walk you through the whole process start to finish.

As you start setting up your software, consider the key back-end settings needing attention for user experience, branding and functionality. Within your WordPress dashboard, start by deleting sample posts and pages from your theme under Pages > All Pages to begin with a blank site. Add a polished "Home" page and initial site sections through adding new pages, structuring your site hierarchy.

From here, navigate to Settings > General Settings to review options for titling your site, tagline, administrator email, timezone and date formats. Update these details to capture your blog brand and locale accurately right away. Double check that permalink settings utilize Post Name identifiers for SEO friendliness as well.

Venture to Settings > Media Settings to configure image sizes, thumbnail options and storage location on server for your visual assets. Determine what maximum image widths and heights suit your content display needs, generating corresponding Medium Large image presets. Enable automatic image resizing on upload for responsive design too.

Finally, navigate to Settings > Discussion Settings to make decisions on comment functionalities, email notifications and social media. Enable pingbacks and trackbacks to keep conversations flowing across posts and sites by notifying you when others link to your content while opting into email alerts about new comments to stay looped in.

With your domain connected and site settings personalized to your brand, audience and functionality preferences, the technical foundations for providing an optimized reader experience are in place. Maintain this attentiveness to site configuration details, plugins and user testing as you continue maturing your blog over time. Consider site management just as vital for growth as your content itself, facilitating deeper reader connections through your digital environment.

CHAPTER 2

Producing Quality Blog Content

Behind every great blog post lies extensive research and strategic planning to deeply understand your niche audience and craft content that resonates. Rather than arbitrarily picking topics, implement a research-based content planning methodology that ensures you publish informed, relevant posts perfectly matched to your reader's interests and questions.

Start developing razor-sharp understanding of your target reader through social listening across social media groups, forums, Quora, Reddit and any niche communities your audience gathers. Immerse yourself in conversations to grasp their language patterns, current challenges, goals, questions and needs. Maintain an ongoing content idea bank capturing any information gaps, issues begging solutions or recurring themes you uncover.

Complement social engagement with keyword research using tools like Ahrefs, SEMRush and Google Keyword Planner to reveal high-potential topics and terms your niche actively searches but finds little valuable information around currently. Unearth keyword opportunity gems with sufficient volume but relatively low competition for likely viral potential once you address the need.

Armed with extensive audience insights and keyword data, create an editorial calendar template to methodically structure planned publication dates and topics in alignment to seasons, events, awareness months and other considerations that dictate relevancy timing. Categorize content across evergreen fundamentals versus trends requiring timelier posts so you balance informational staples with content keyed into current events.

For example, an education blogger may plan certain evergreen posts explaining fundamentals of curriculum design and learning psychology while slotting timely trend pieces around back-to-school preparation tips or coping with pandemic disruptions. Use your calendar to guarantee you balance broad appeal evergreens with traffic-spiking trend stories.

With your publishing schedule set, shift to intensive individual post research and planning using in-depth outline templates examining angles like:

- Hook - What fresh perspective or unique personal experience are you bringing readers hooked by an intriguing opening?

- Overview - What content structure, key points and flow will comprehensively educate readers on this topic?

- Visuals - What types of images, graphics or multimedia help demonstrate concepts visually?

- Conclusions - How will you recap takeaways and transition readers to related topics for further learning?

- Promotions - What social media caption snippets or intriguing questions generate shares?

Through dedicating time to research audience interests, optimizing keyword selections and engineering outlines ensuring 360-degree topic coverage, you produce posts delivering truly fulfilling value. These efforts build authority and loyalty over simply chasing vanity metrics like pageviews through clickbait or algorithms.

Yes, rigorous audience research, planning and outlining requires extensive investment - potentially hours per post. But these practices directly translate to higher-converting visitors as your Laser targeted message resonance and thorough answers earn you perfect search result rankings and referrals. Think quality over quantity, gradually scaling output after nailing your value proposition, voice and positioning first.

Feedback loops with your audience also prove invaluable for aligning to their needs over time as you ask about their burning questions, conduct surveys on topics of interest and learn directly from comments or emails. Always refresh plans to match their evolving needs rather than assumptions.

By constantly expanding niche knowledge and designing high ROI content journeys for your readers rather than lone posts in isolation, you become an indispensable guide over transient blogger. Achieve this trust through the meticulous planning and research separating experts from armchair commentators.

Creating Compelling Headlines and Blog Posts

In an era of endless online distractions vying for reader attention, creating compelling headlines and blog posts that immediately capture interest separates thriving sites from invisible blogs. Rather than prioritizing keywords or awkwardly jamming concepts together, take an audience-centric approach to craft messages oozing relevance and intrigue for your niche.

Start by selecting themes and framing rooted in reader emotions, struggles, goals and the language they naturally use when discussing a topic. This might mean headline phrasing like "Overwhelmed Working Moms Reveal Time-Saving School Morning Routines" or "How Introverts Can Overcome Anxiety to Finally Make Friends". Specify the exact reader profiles and feelings your content promises to address.

Powerful headline formulas include:

1. Numbered Lists - Top 7 Mistakes When Caring for Orchids
2. How To Guides - How I Learned to Stop Procrastinating in Under 1 Week
3. Weird Facts - Scientists Reveal Surprising Impact Eating Celery Has on Memory

4. Common Questions - Why Do Some Runners Hit a Performance Plateau?

Skim forums and social platforms related to your niche to note the types of casual language, shorthand and terminology your audience uses when talking about a topic. Integrate these native phrases seamlessly into headlines and posts rather than formal jargon unlikely said aloud.

For example, fashion bloggers reference trends by nicknames like using "athleisure" instead of "activewear" or gamers say "grinding" rather than the formal "gaining experience points". Matching native reader vocabulary levels up trust and rapport quickly compared to misaligned language.

Even more vital than perfectly worded headlines lies crafting posts delivering on reader expectations while simultaneously surprising them with unexpected insights. Structure flows moving from what readers likely already know on a topic into novel analysis, contrarian viewpoints or uncommon frameworks that jolt them to attention.

A post on mindfulness meditation could overview what it involves initially before transitioning into lesser discussed elements like precisely how mindfulness changes the brain. A book review might provide brief objective summary before pivoting into uncommon critique on prose weaknesses other reviews overlook.

Deploy cliffhanger chapter endings, weave personal stories, pose thoughtful discussion questions and infuse personality across posts through these avenues that shatter generic advice association, keeping visitors glued sentence-by-sentence. Treat posts as lively conversations where readers excitedly wonder "What's next??" after each paragraph, not textbooks dryly lecturing them.

Record your screen narrating draft posts aloud to hear where sections lack vocal enthusiasm or drag on listlessly so you can punch up wording. Read the first and last lines of each paragraph - where momentum dips, rewrite entire sections. Carry intimate passion into even technical posts through conversational tone and intriguing narrative approaches likely missing currently.

Through tantalizing headlines promising what readers desperately want and posts overdelivering exceptionally captivating value, you claim sticky positioning in their hearts and browsing habits over fleeting content they instantly forget. Match Mission orientation with word mastery and you possess the key ingredients for compulsively readable posts.

Optimizing Posts for Search Engines

Strategic Techniques for Optimizing Your Blog Content to Rank Highly in Search Engines

While great writing and insight ensures remarkable blog content, optimizing posts specifically for high visibility across search engines like Google determines if anyone actually finds your wisdom in the first place. By engineering key elements on-page and structuring content for machines and readers alike, your content ascends rankings bringing sustainable organic traffic.

Start by conducting detailed keyword research through tools like Ahrefs, Moz and SEMrush on low competition yet sufficiently searched terms and questions to base posts around. Aligning closely to what real people search transfers relevance signals to search bots who then prominently feature your content. But avoid awkwardly over-optimizing or keyword stuffing as Google's algorithms now detect such manipulation.

Expand beyond just head keywords to holistically optimize topics through Title tags, URL structures, meta descriptions, image alt text, related keywords, explanatory links, tags and more that all filter relevance to search bots. Permalink settings should utilize Post Name identifiers for clean URLs with primary head terms included.

For example, a post entitled "8 Morning Stretches to Reduce Back Pain" would optimize keywords across areas:

- Title Tag: 8 Best Morning Stretches to Relieve and Prevent Back Pain
- URL Slug: /morning-stretches-reduce-back-pain

- Meta Description: Start your days pain-free by practicing these 8 physician-approved morning stretches proven to align your spine, improve posture and prevent back pain all day.

- alt Text: Person doing morning stretch exercise to relieve back pain

- Related Keywords: upper back stretches, stretches for lower back pain, back pain exercises

- And Tags: back pain, back stretches, morning routines, pain relief exercises

Section content flows using explanatory paragraph transitions introducing next critical subtopics around a core term for smooth relevancy: "Now that we've covered spine alignment basics, let's discuss optimal posture stretches to include in morning routines".

Additionally, format posts appealingly for both readers and search bots through ample whitespace, strategic bolding rather than ALL CAPS, labeled section headers summarizing following paragraphs, table of contents plugins for longer guides, bulleted takeaways and more. Images and videos boost rankings so long as you describe them accessibly through captions.

Interlink related site content extensively through natural mentions across posts to multiply relevance signals around connected topics: "As discussed in our accessory guide for beginner runners, moisture wicking socks prevent blisters". Tag these links to actual posts for added context.

Promote new content across social media channels upon publishing not only to drive referral traffic but further notify Google of fresh relevance signals to evaluate. Encourage early commenters and link sharers to accelerate initial search visibility through this immediate engagement.

By holistically optimizing posts for seamless reader consumption and savvy backend engineering specifically for search bots verbatim analyzing your content, you massively scale discoverability. Treat SEO as integral authoring ingredient separating findable guides from practically invisible blogs.

Developing Your Writing Skills

Regardless of your current skill level, seeking continual growth through dedicated practice ultimately determines blogging excellence. Rather than coasting on any modest early praise, commit to sharpening writing and communication mastery over years through these insights for unlocking greater impact.

Start by voraciously studying bestselling authors, viral blogs and captivating speakers across niches to analyze what makes their voice, framing and style so alluring. Deconstruct their sentence structure, paragraph flow, vocabulary, use of descriptive details, humor and transition techniques stealing attention word after word.

Discover what universal elements underpin their emotional resonance and reading smoothness for integration into your own expression in authentic ways. Perhaps you adopt the short, fragmented phrasing of modern media while layering in classical rhetorical cues. Build your unique writing DNA combining influences that clicks with readers.

Alongside analyzing outside voices, dedicate consistent time to actually writing daily without self-judgement to ease perfectionist tendencies stifling progress. Set a timer for 10-15 minutes daily to just pour unfiltered words onto paper or screen capturing whatever arises mentally. Writing begets writing -

simply showing up consistently builds momentum.

Voracious reading across diverse topics also expands writerly knowledge, vocabulary and conversational tone infinitely more than any course. Digest newspaper longforms, philosophical treatises, scientific American journals and numerous blogs weekly while noting compelling passages. Reading quality heightens writing quality over time indirectly through unconscious absorption.

When drafting posts, read aloud to catch clumsy phrasing as our ears detect awkwardness our eyes may gloss over while editing. If a sentence meanders or lacks clarity when spoken, rewrite it utilizing the techniques of admired writers. Recording passages to play back amplifies this effect further.

Seed early drafts of articles with friends or colleagues open to providing candid feedback about sections losing their attention or lacking conviction. Welcome critiques on areas needing punchier framing, tighter editing, additional research or reworked structure to heighten clarity.

Polish the rhythmic flow between sentences and tighten transitional flow from paragraph to paragraph. Eliminate generic filler words diluting writing power like "very", "really" or "in order to", forcing more descriptive language instead through thesaurus study.

Finally, widen creative horizons studying song lyrics, speeches, poetry and improvisational comedy for their distillation of potent messages people remember verbatim. Master word economy while tapping emotion - what hidden writing gems exist in other mediums? Infuse writing with this blend of concision, evocation and conversational fluidity.

Through dedicated reading, daily writing habits, embracing feedback and analyzing the masters across fields, the building blocks for resonating reader impact assemble over time. Writing excellence stems not from fleeting inspiration but habitual honing of the 10,000 hour rule. Step forward daily in craft dedication on this lifelong path.

CHAPTER 3

Building an Audience and Community

Promoting Your Blog Content

Beyond publishing remarkable writing, intentionally promoting posts directly correlates to audience growth as new visitors discover your insights through social media, email, collaborations and more. Build multi-channel promotional systems reaching fans and influencers likely to share worthy posts if they see them.

Start by enabling social sharing buttons prominently on all articles and site pages through WordPress plugins like AddThis. At minimum, include user-friendly click buttons for Twitter, Facebook, Pinterest and LinkedIn to lower barriers letting enthusiastic readers spread your wisdom instantly with one click.

Expand sharing channels even further through browser extensions like Shareaholic installing additional one-click sharing functionality for SMS texts, emails and hundreds of other networks. The easier you make amplifying your ideas for others, the faster exposure accelerates.

With frictionless sharing options implemented site-wide, shift to crafting irresistibly shareable custom messages within your social media channels when announcing new articles. Study viral blogs in your niche and model their snippet craft - what post preview language piques your click impulse immediately?

For example, a fashion blog may tweet new posts starting with: "Have jeans but nothing to wear? Here's 5 fresh fall looks under $50 that elevate those denim staples..." This preview sparks instant curiosity and action rather than blandly saying: "New blog post on fall outfit ideas". Speak directly in second person to the precise reader profiles most compelled.

Track when your audience is most active on social channels and send alerts when new content goes lives during these high visibility windows for their timezones. Post consistently 2-3 times daily sharing articles, intriguing questions and conversations - not just during new launches. Rhythmically engage audiences through varied value touches that multiply organic reach.

Offsite, develop relationships with relevant niche websites, industry hubs and blogs open to syndicating your articles or publishing guest contributions backlinking to your site. Target sites frequented by your ideal readers but cover complementary rather than competing content so partnerships drive shared growth.

Proactively pitch original pieces or repurposed/expanded content from popular posts to site admins or use guest posting services like MyBlogGuest, BlogDash and GuestPostTracker connecting bloggers to backlinking opportunities. Ensure you provide genuine value, not spammy pitches, when requesting republication.

Finally, interlink content and sites extensively when references naturally enhance pieces for readers. For example, mentioning related reviews, comparative posts or foundational primers you've written previously. Outbound linking to niche websites also builds authority and goodwill through additional references.

With multi-channel promotion constantly feeding your content to fresh networked pools of potential fans, your ideas find the audiences they deserve. Combine optimized messaging, strategic timing and collaboration to sustain awareness growth long-term.

Growing Your Email Subscriber List

While social media and search provide blog traffic surges, collecting loyal subscribers through email newsletter signup incentives converts casual visitors into devoted recurring fans. Offering exclusive value, discounts or insider updates readers can't get anywhere else captures contacts infinitely more profitable than fickle social media followers.

Install user-friendly email signup forms at the top and bottom of blog pages through WordPress plugins like ConvertKit or Mailchimp. Allow readers to easily subscribe on site rather than forcing uncomfortable social follow hoops first. Many visitors desire to follow anonymously initially before publicly aligning so enable this.

Entice email signups by promoting "subscriber-only" bonus offers like special reports, discounts, early previews, contests, giveaways and other elite perks just for your list. For example, a food blogger might promise subscribers early access to coveted secret recipes. A book reviewer could email advance previews of works not yet released.

Make offers explicitly exclusive and high-value to overcome assumption barriers that signups primarily deliver annoying spam rather than VIP treatment. State exactly what beloved subscriber rewards come with joining compared to social followers lacking this insider access.

Strategically place signup call-to-actions at the end of posts after you've demonstrated immense value already through stellar content. Once they realize the quality insights they'll get regularly, most visitors happily trade emails for more of your game-changing wisdom rather than random interrupting pop-ups demanding contacts prematurely.

Send a brief, welcoming email to new subscribers instantly thanking them for joining and introducing some popular evergreen posts to check out. Quickly reward signups so they feel special treatment right away compared to cold social stats.

Separate from promotions, actively survey what exclusive content offerings subscribers want like special edition newsletters, personalized advice hours, niche community forums and other ideas they suggest. Co-create together the elite membership site benefits subsidizing their dedication.

Through respectfully offering, not aggressively demanding, email contacts in return for genuinely high-value newsletter content, you convert fleeting visitors into ideal clients for your knowledge. Long-term loyalty and maximal customer lifetime value stem from personalized email relationships not commoditized social media masses.

Interacting With Readers Through Comments

Beyond simply publishing quality content, savvy bloggers actively participate in comment sections daily as pivotal touchpoints cementing reader loyalty and trust over the long term. Rather than treating discussions as obligatory afterthoughts, dedicate time responding respectfully, asking thoughtful follow-up questions, and steering conversations towards constructive territory.

Start by checking and thoughtfully replying to comments daily rather than allowing them to pile up endlessly unaddressed. Set calendar reminders if necessary to prevent this vital community task from slipping through the cracks when you get busy. Even a simple "Thanks for reading, Jenny!" personalization signals to readers their perspectives don't disappear into an empty void, ignored.

Move beyond generic thanks to demonstrate you truly read comments fully before responding. Seek to accurately understand contexts and sentiment to avoid misunderstood, blanket reactions. Ask clarifying questions if you're unsure specific facets, or need additional details to provide quality guidance.

For example, receive a comment like: "As a new mother struggling with anxiety, I found this article really invalidating and overly simplified..."

You could reply: "Thanks for your openness sharing your experience here. As a new mom still learning myself, I'd love to understand more about why this piece felt invalidating so I can better support the complex emotions motherhood involves. Are there any resources or perspectives that have helped you navigate parenting/anxiety you'd recommend?"

This respectfully affirms your genuine interest hearing more rather than rapid-firing automated-seeming thanks liable to aggravate tensions already elevated. Demonstrating earnest attention earns surprising dividends unearthing audience needs future content can address too.

Pay extra care responding to critiques, concerns or corrections avoiding initial defensive reactions. Start by acknowledging their perspective and feelings before adding additional context around decisions that may explain your intentions better. Diffuse rather than dismiss.

For example, receiving accusations around insensitive or controversial stances warrants replies like:

"I appreciate you raising these concerns directly. Allow me to clarify my personal experience on the topic..." Then explain respectfully rather than attacking criticisms as personal attacks eroding community trust.

Ask followers clarifying questions on critiques you genuinely don't fully grasp yet, to understand objections better before responding. This humble learning approach centers your community's experiences first.

If discussions still degrade into unconstructive arguments anyway, respectfully yet firmly moderate by reiterating your intentions for peaceful conversation but unwillingness to tolerate personal attacks or slander eroding community trust. Then politely disengage rather than pouring flames.

Consider directly addressing hot-button issues likely to spark debate in post scripts or comment disclaimers, linking your values to content decisions. Transparently explain niche perspectives seemingly excluded, your personal limitations to give advice, conflicts of interest and other disclosures that reduce misinterpretations.

For example, a finance blogger could write: "This post focuses specifically on credit card point systems which I have close experience with. I fully acknowledge the privileges and barriers involved in credit access depending on identity and circumstance, though those important discussions exceed my direct expertise presently."

Overall, vibrant comment sections demonstrating you truly care about reader reactions, questions and even uncertainties around your content earn surprising loyalty dividends over time. Dedicate resources fostering an inclusive tone welcoming new voices different than your own. Readers lingering on sites facilitating meaningful peer exchanges stick around buying journeys far longer than just fleeting posts or content, exponentially boosting value delivered.

Leveraging on Social Media Effectively

While your blog itself remains the mothership broadcasting your best insights, strategically leveraging social media multiplies awareness beyond niche corners of the internet into mainstream visibility. Rather than constantly promoting content though, balance self-promotion with truly valuable engagement.

Start by determining the 1-3 primary platforms where your target audience and influencers already actively spend time socializing online. Save yourself stretched-thin frustration trying to maintain a presence everywhere. Actively listen first to discover where discussions around your topics frequent, then consistently participate.

For example, ambitious entrepreneurs often concentrate on LinkedIn, Twitter and medium-specific platforms like BiggerPockets for real estate investors. Opposingly, teens obsess over youth-dominated platforms like Snapchat, TikTok and Instagram. Meet audiences where they cluster digitally.

With your key channels identified, devote time daily intermingling promotional, curational and conversational style posts attracting those disinterested in straight blog pitches. Share relevant industry articles, pose engaging questions, highlight resources and consult followers as needed between mentions of your newest insights.

For example, a recipe blogger cultivates genuine value on Instagram through gorgeous food photography inspiration, ingredient substitutions guidance responding to comment questions and only occasional new recipe alerts to their latest site offerings. Follow the 80/20 engagement/promotion ratio ensuring audiences feel supported daily, not marketed at.

Strategically tag industry influencers, potential collaborative partners and niche hashtags even within everyday social posts to widen visibility by piggybacking trending conversations. Move beyond isolated blogger soliloquies - fuse into diverse communities already active discussing common interests.

Research optimal posting times and intervals for each platform using social media tools like Buffer or Hootsuite determining when your audiences monitor updates most actively. Don't bombard sleeping timelines. Analyze engagement analytics to guide sharing schedules towards maximized exposure.

Follow niche leaders, potential partners, engaged commenters and collaborators to build reciprocal community connections, not just accumulate vanity metrics through one-sided follower gathering. Prioritize gradual genuine relationship development through ongoing value.

Instead of purely push-style broadcasting, pull followers into interactive dialogue through questions, polls and open-ended calls for their experiences on topics you discuss. This community co-creation approach multiplies engagement and retention over isolated posts vanishing in feeds.

With a balanced infusion of industry immersion, audience co-creation and valuable curation separating you from pure promotional spam, social media drives site traffic more sustainably than trigger-happy link blasts alone ever could. Meet audiences through consistent participation in their communities first, positioned as peer helper before hardselling people unfamiliar with your knowledge support still. Patiently earn trust through steady insight sharing tailored to each platform's culture and expectations.

CHAPTER 4

Monetizing Your Blog

Basic Options Like Ads and Affiliates

Beyond just sharing your passion, transforming blogging into a profitable business supporting your work requires implementing basic yet versatile income streams like advertising and affiliate programs. While seemingly simple, excelling at these monetization building blocks through tailored optimization significantly impacts income scaling.

Start by installing free ad placements through Google Adsense allowing text, image and video ads to display contextually across your site. By registering your blog with this network giant boasting over 90% of global digital ad market share, Google automatically determines suitable sponsors and handles ad serving technologically.

You control layout preferences for positioning ad blocks in sidebars, within content or article footers while Google controls actual advertisers and relevancy. They provide site coding to embed or plugins through WordPress simplifying setup like WP Adsense Auto Ads configuring everything automatically.

With platforms installed, boost earnings by fine-tuning category exclusions if some promoted products don't suit your brand. For example, a children's site avoids alcohol sponsorship. Additionally, target geographic preferences to your highest-value reader demographics.

Google optimizes relevance automatically, though you can blacklist repeatedly poor-performing ads dragging down overall revenue through your account dashboard while allowing new sponsors through the extensive platform.

Beyond Adsense, explore niche-specific advertising networks like BuySellAds for financial blogs or Mediavine serving lifestyle sites. These players promise superior specialization and often outearn generic networks significantly, especially at scale above 100,000 monthly views.

Now to affiliate marketing, explore commissions promoting relevant products, services and even other sites through tracked referral links that pay you transparently per conversion. Amazon Associates likely proves the largest, most varied product catalog with baseline 4-10% sales commissions in addition to bonuses for volume.

Before plastering links arbitrarily however, vet products thoroughly ensuring legitimate quality customers actually desire. Share items organically helpful for reader needs. Disclose affiliate relationships transparently to establish community trust that you recommend based on utility, not payments alone.

Share a variety of affiliate links contextually in posts when mentioning related tools, rather than isolating monetization sections awkwardly. For example:

"This stainless steel garlic press makes home cooking prepping easier with dishwasher safe cleaning too (Amazon link). Now onto our next kitchen time saver - the innovative chopper I'm loving for fast veggie prep..."

Track affiliate link performance within program dashboards to double down on highest-converting products while removing poor performers over time. Considering signing up multiple supportive affiliate programs beyond Amazon like ShareASale housing major brands spanning fashion, software, educational tools and much more so no referral opportunities are missed.

Through fine-tuning contextual ad placements and strategically recommending affiliate products naturally supplementing blog content, you cash in on alignment between reader needs and sponsor solutions that deliver persistent income. Though simple, mastering maximally relevant ads and selectively shared offerings sets the table for monetizing attention into earnings.

Offering Paid Subscriptions

Introducing paid subscriptions can be a lucrative way to monetize your blog. By offering exclusive, members-only content and perks for a monthly or yearly fee, you create an additional revenue stream beyond display ads and affiliate marketing. However, it requires considering your audience, goals, and resources when structuring your subscription service.

Assessing Your Blog and Audience

Before launching subscriptions, determine if paid content aligns with your blog's overall direction and readership. Consider these key questions:

What is my niche? Finance blogs, for example, tend to do better with subscriptions than hobby blogs. Identify if exclusive analysis or professional expertise could entice subscribers.

Who is currently visiting my blog? Evaluate traffic sources and demographic data. For instance, social media-driven food blogs often translate better into ad revenues than paid plans due to audience interests.

Does my content provide "must-have" value? Specialized knowledge and reporting requiring heavy time investments on your end tends to drive more subscription loyalty versus readily available information.

Gauge overall demand by surveying your email list and social media followers. Research competing blogs' subscription formats as well to identify price points and feature expectations.

Structuring Your Paid Subscription Offering

Once committing to paid subscriptions, you must determine the right framework and features.

Membership Levels

Offer different tiers based on access granted. For example:

1. Bronze ($5 per month): entry-level with some exclusive posts or newsletter access
2. Silver ($10 per month): all bronze benefits plus extended content like special reports
3. Gold ($20 per month): all silver benefits plus direct inquiry capabilities, special events invites, etc.

Presenting clearly differentiated levels allows segmenting your audience willingness-to-pay. It also remains scalable, letting you add higher tiers later for premium positioning.

Specialized Content Types

Consider content to place behind the paywall:

- Long-form analyses: In-depth investigations, expert interviews, market sizing models for industry topics

- Downloadable templates, worksheets or audio: Let Gold memberships download your popular blogging templates or exclusive podcast episodes to listen offline

- Member forums and direct access: Foster an exclusive community. Allow direct access to subject matter experts like financial advisors or fitness instructors for niche blogs.

- Behind-the-scenes or story insight: Offer additional commentary, drafts or access like monthly video hangouts to enrich perspective.

- Clearly highlight exclusive content and perks in all membership descriptions. Continually add new locked posts and resources so members get ongoing additional value above free posts.

Technology Set Up

Leveraging the right software platforms streamlines delivering paid subscriptions:

Membership plugins: Use established plugins like MemberPress or membership solutions from Patreon or Buy Me A Coffee for subscription management capabilities.

Email service integration: Connect your email marketing platform to membership software for tailored, subscriber-only emails.

Membership portals: Provide exclusive web portals for subscribers away from your main blog feed to emphasize value.

Ensure you adequately support payment processing and access restrictions based on subscription level.

Promoting Paid Subscriptions

Now comes driving paid sign-ups through clear messaging and promotions:

Homepage headers: Place subscription details in global headers so all visitors immediately see offerings.

Sidebar features: Keep subscription details constantly visible via sidebar or site footer banners with links to membership pages.

Blog post calls-to-action: Insert CTA copy and buttons in blog posts to capture reader interest for premium content.

Free trial periods: Offer free 7-day trials to provide a risk-free initiation point.

Loyalty discounts: Reward long-time free subscribers with special promo codes for bigger savings on initial paid sign-ups.

Email list outreach: Utilize pop-ups and dedicated emails to email list highlighting subscriptions. Offer initial discounts for acting fast.

Continually test language, pricing and formats using analytics to optimize conversions. Survey members also to identify future subscriptions they would be interested in.

Driving Paid Blog Subscriptions

Implementing paid subscriptions necessitates planning regarding technology, content and promotions. But blogger-to-reader exclusivity can prove highly lucrative. Specialized, premium content and access drives subscriber loyalty over time. Paid models ultimately let you make blogging itself more sustainable by complementing other monetization approaches. With the right research and execution, subscription revenue can become a primary income stream.

Launching a membership site

Creating an engaging membership site allows you to generate recurring revenue while providing exclusive value to a defined community. By charging monthly or annual fees, members gain access to restricted content and perks unavailable to non-paying site visitors.

If structured strategically, membership sites can become lucrative, but they require careful planning and execution across technology, user experience, and marketing. Follow these best practices for launching a paid membership site successfully:

Assess Content and Offerings

Start by conducting self-audits of existing assets and future content pipelines that could support members. Identify topics and access of highest value. Can you offer downloadable guides, direct expert access, virtual meetups or behind-the-scenes commentary? Outline concrete offerings and consider various subscription tiers based on depth of access granted. Survey existing audiences for feature wish lists to validate direction.

Choose a CMS Platform

Select an appropriate content management system (CMS) for seamlessly managing members and restricting access based on subscription levels. WordPress paired with plug-ins like MemberPress facilitates secure registration portals, membership profiles, subscription payments and content restrictions. Alternatively, all-in-one services like Mighty Networks or Circle provide tailored community and membership features out-of-the-box. Ensure your platform makes adding new content, messaging members, and tracking analytics simple from one dashboard.

Set Up Payments and Access

Now integrate payment processing and access controls. Choose payment partners that allow offering coupons or usage across global customer bases and enable instant access upon completed purchases. Use single sign-on integrations so members can easily login via Google or Facebook and not manage multiple accounts. Provide self-service account management portals for updating payment methods and subscription levels at any time.

Build Exclusive Community Architecture

Design an intuitive yet exclusive members-only architecture separate from your public website. Provide a special corner for members through a pop-up portal on your homepage for sneak peek community access. Develop a full-fledged separate members dashboard area housing locked posts, member profiles, discussion forums and event calendars. Highlight with branding, colors and messaging emphasizing the exclusive nature of all offerings.

Market Site Launch

Spread the word leading up to launch by teasing exclusive features and special introductory pricing to current audiences. Send a series of emails to website subscribers emphasizing special early member registration deals. Promote launch via social media channels and through partnerships, contests or affiliates incentives to facilitate initial sign-ups.

The key to ongoing subscription renewals lies in enhancing membership perceived value over time. Commit to releasing new locked posts, training programs, or virtual meetups on a consistent basis. Implement member surveys and monitor community forum talks for new feature requests. Consider adding higher-tier offerings as well for premium positioning. Successful membership sites continually mold experiences to align with target member interests across lifecycles.

Install web analytics tools for monitoring key metrics like monthly recurring revenue (MRR), churn rates and content consumption trends. Identify best-converting offers through A/B testing introduction prices and sales copy lingo. Determine most engaged member segments and double down on content tailored for those groups. Continually refine to maximize customer lifetime value.

Creating compelling membership destinations requires aligning technology and content with community-building. But the recurring income and audience connection such sites facilitate make the effort worthwhile. Follow the above steps for ensuring your membership community vision has all ingredients for success before launch.

CHAPTER 5

Becoming a Successful Blogger

Turning blogging into a business

Many bloggers start out writing as a hobby or to build their personal brand. But as your readership grows, generating an income from your blog can become a viable pursuit, whether supplemental revenue or even a full-time business.

With strategic business planning and monetization approaches, you transform a hobby website into a highly profitable media property. Follow these key steps for turning your blog into a money-making business:

Refine Your Blog's Niche and Positioning

As bloggers attract bigger audiences over time, opportunities arise for tailoring content more narrowly to engage specific, passionate reader segments. Conduct an audit of top performing articles and throttle in on recurring high-interest themes ripe for targeting.

For example, digital marketing blogs might identify SEO strategies as a breakout reader favorite to double down on, spinning off niche sites specifically SEO focused. Outdoors blogs might spot gear reviews as consistent traffic drivers warranting a more dedicated backpacking gear site.

Clearly communicate updated positioning to readers while directing legacy content to new sister sites. Updated niche focus allows honing your service offerings and monetization avenues.

Formalize Your Content Production Systems

Treat blogging like a business by implementing formal planning and development systems for managing content. Outline quarterly editorial calendars complete with article ideas, themes to cover, and specific blog post requirements. Maintain organized spreadsheets of past coverage and emerging stories to fuel future ideation.

Structure work weeks around defined blogging deliverables and deadlines to establish consistent output procedures. Set goals for metrics like annual posts needed, revenue targets required per piece and reader engagement objectives to work towards. Formal systems enable productivity scaling.

Diversify Monetization Models

Every sizeable blog should incorporate a diversified income mix, including:

Display Advertising – Install site-wide platforms like Google Ad Manager for automating placement of relevant text and image ads across all pages based on page content. Display delivers reliable revenue.

Affiliate Marketing Links – Incorporate contextual affiliate links to referenced products within posts. When readers click and buy, you earn affiliate commissions.

Sponsored Posts – Sell dedicated posts to advertisers wanting custom content showcasing offerings for target audiences. Develop sponsorship sales sheets detailing blog metrics and reader demographics for pitching.

Paid Subscriptions – Offer exclusive member access to premium content and community experiences via paid subscriptions you manage through third-party platforms.

Expanded offerings and revenue diversification make income potential more recession-proof and deliver compounding returns.

Develop Products and Services

Leverage your position and audience to develop additional monetized offerings:

Paid newsletters – Upsell readers into premium editions for exclusive analysis.

Online courses – Structure your expertise into virtual classes and credential programs.

In-person events – Host local meetup groups or larger conferences to facilitate networking opportunities between your community.

Merchandise – Sell branded apparel, accessories and gear representing your niche angle.

Consulting or coaching – Help brands directly with services informed by your industry experience.

Products and services establish multiple customer touchpoints while letting readers engage deeper with content they already love.

Hire Supporting Staff

As income scales, enlist support staff to lighten workloads, including:

Blog managers - Help coordinate planning, editing, production and distribution across all channels.

Sales specialists - Prospect sponsors, facilitate product fulfillment orders and manage campaign execution.

Community coordinators - Oversee newsletter delivery, forum discussions and event programming.

Outsource contractors – Assign graphic design, web development or virtual assistance tasks to trusted freelancers for added bandwidth.

Delegating responsibilities to dedicated personnel lets bloggers focus purely on content while ensuring smooth operations across all facets of the business.

Formalize Legal and Finance

With income scaling significantly, formally register your business identity complete with tax structuring optimized for revenue streams like freelance writing fees or digital products sales.

Consult lawyers on best entity status options– like LLCs or S-corps – to protect personal assets and tap into additional tax deductions for expenses like equipment purchases or home office use.

Implement small business accounting software and work with financial advisors for managing taxes appropriately across national, state and local jurisdictions based on service areas and employees. Following sound financial practices keeps blogging profits tidy as income snowballs.

The Evolution to a Media Company

While launching a blog once required just web hosting and a passion for writing, transforming into a thriving media business necessitates implementing systems for formal planning, distribution, operations, finance, sales and community engagement. But with the right strategic foundations and effort, bloggers can steadily evolve website properties into diversified, sustainable commercial enterprises.

So approach your content venture with a long-term business mindset from the outset. Stay focused on enhancing infrastructure and processes over chasing quick wins. With consistency comes growth in audience, influence and income. Before you know it, you'll be running a fully fledged and dynamic digital media company.

Creating an Editorial Calendar For Consistency

Building an Editorial Calendar for a Productive Blogging Strategy

Maintaining a consistent blogging schedule bolsters search visibility, reader loyalty and revenue opportunities. But producing quality content across multiple channels on a regular timeline requires strategic planning. This is where implementing an editorial calendar becomes vital.

An editorial calendar provides an overview of what you will create and publish on your blog over a set period of time, often monthly or quarterly. Mapping articles and themes in advance enables sticking to posting cadences, allocates resources efficiently and spotlights content gaps to fill.

Follow these best practices for structuring an actionable blogging editorial calendar:

Outline Planning Horizons

First determine relevant content planning horizons. Monthly editorial calendars allow close-range scheduling helpful for prolific posting rates of 20+ pieces a month. Quarterly calendars provide longer-term direction better suited for blogs on 1-2 times a week schedules.

Match the advance planning duration to your website's current activity levels. This spotlight areas needing more ideas to sustain pipelines while giving flexibility to plug-in topical stories as they emerge.

Audit Past Content

Conduct an audit of recent blog coverage and metrics to inform calendar direction. Review past 12 months of posts and highlight:

- Top performing pieces based on traffic and engagement
- Evergreen green content continually driving organic search
- Seasonal content tied to annual events or trends
- Underperforming topics to eliminate or refresh

Assess what content resonates while strategizing evergreen refreshes and new or expanded seasonal themes that outperform.

Brainstorm Topic Ideas

Maintain an ongoing spreadsheet of "Blog Post Ideas" to tap for editorial calendar population. Jot down ideas as they arise from current events, reader or client conversations, or trends you spot across your niche. Tag notes by categories, themes, formats or difficulty to facilitate sorting.

When calendar planning time comes, review and filter idea list into specific posts for drafting, factoring in target metrics and resources needs per piece. Populate into designated calendar dates.

Allocate Writing and Promotion Resources

With target posts outlined, identify team members responsible for creating each piece, including writers, designers, editors and strategists. Also denote key steps with owners and timelines for ancillary activities like image purchases, quote requests or research checkpoints.

Building in ownership structure keeps projects moving while letting managers customize support based on individual workloads and strengths.

Plot Promotional Channels

Integrate promotional channels like social media, email newsletters and paid amplification into the calendar alongside necessary content. Identify relevant maker days, awareness events or hashtag trends suited for specific posts to align with for extra exposure potential.

Design promotional templates like tweets or pins when planning each piece to streamline distribution support immediately at publish. Advanced thought on supplementary activities beyond publish boosts content reach.

Continually Optimize and Refresh

Monitor metrics for each piece listed in the calendar post-distribution to assess performance. Identify recurring themes or topics that over-index as reader favorites warranting additional coverage. Assess areas underperforming expectations that necessitate new creative directions or phasing out.

Regularly refresh your editorial calendars every quarter or annually based on insights learned for strengthening future content programming and consistency.

An editorial calendar acts as the blueprint for executing an intentional blogging strategy built upon your audience interests, resources and business goals. Detailed calendars transform haphazard ideation into reliable pipelines enabling consistent value delivery to readers. Consistency powers audience growth and revenue scaling over time.

Tracking analytics and growth

Building a successful blog requires more than quality writing alone. You must actively track performance data to spot content trends, pinpoint growth opportunities and outline improvement strategies. From traffic to engagement to income biomarkers, quantifying your blog's health through analytics is essential.

Implement these best practices for monitoring essential blog metrics and maximizing expansion:

Install Analytics Tracking

The first step entails installing a web analytics platform like Google Analytics or Adobe Analytics for monitoring engagement and outcomes. Tracking code implementation enables recording key activities like:

- Traffic sources driving visits
- Post and page view volumes
- Referral pathways users take
- On-page behaviors like clicks or scroll depth
- Conversion events like downloads or purchases

Anchor all strategy decisions to observe analytics rather than assumptions or vanity metrics like social media follows. Platforms like Google Analytics offer free yet powerful capabilities for segmenting and visualizing data around both audiences and content.

Determine Core Metrics

With analytics installed, identify metrics most vital for informing content and commercial decisions. Differentiate between vanity metrics like social media shares that do not directly correlate to outcomes vs. performance metrics like email list growth and sales reflecting real impact.

Examples of core metrics to consistently track include:

- Monthly site users and traffic rates

- Subscriber gain/loss and open rates

- Individual post view counts

- Earnings from merchandise or ad revenue

- ROI for paid promotions or campaigns

Plot the above over time as key performance indicators (KPIs) to spot upward or downward trends requiring intervention.

Set Target Goals

With current baselines established for metrics, set clear goals for future periods to work towards. If currently averaging 50,000 monthly users, establish a goal of 80,000 users by year-end. Use past outcomes to model targets ambitiously yet realistically across areas like email subscribers, organic visits or course Funnel completions.

Compare actuals to targets monthly and re-forecast if needed based on initiative outcomes influencing each metric. Share reports with teams and ensure all activity ladders up to benchmark dashboards.

Identify Optimization Opportunities

Analytics not only quantify overall performance but spotlight specific opportunities for improving results. Review weekly traffic reports to identify both underperforming areas needing adjustment and top trending content to expand upon.

Evaluate completed campaign or initiative data to calculate true impact and ROI. Assess email click through rates by segment to create more personalized messages and template versions.

Continually mine analytics for actionable insights on enhancing content programming, site functionality, promotions and resource allocation.

Treat Analytics as Decision Drivers

Position metrics reports not as vanity summaries but as decision drivers for your blog's overall strategy. Use observed patterns as the impetus for expanding popular sections, phasing out inactive ones redistributing resources to better performing channels or doubling down on formats resonating best with current audiences.

With analytics steering informed, evidence-based decisions instead of guesses, you build a data-driven blogging operation set up for efficient scaling and longevity.

Taking Your Blogging To The Next Level

Launching and maintaining a blog takes significant effort, but the personal brand visibility, audience engagement, and even income potential blogs unlock make the commitment worthwhile. However, growing beyond beginner phases requires actively working towards next level impact and professionalism.

Whether seeking advertising sponsorships, book deals orSpeaking opportunities, elevating perception starts with strategic foundations. Implement these best practices for taking your blogging game to the next level:

Refine Your Unique Blogging Niche

Assess current content and metrics to hone your blog's niche, positioning it more distinctly. Networks expand most organically when centered around specific, clearly defined topics readers cannot find bundled together elsewhere.

For example, an outdoors blog might narrow its angle to focus exclusively on national park camping tips not addressed on generic travel sites. Similarly, a money tips site might specialize solely in financial advice for new parents beyond general personal finance outlets.

Refining niche allows targeting content and community building more precisely. Communicate adjustments through updated branding and messaging across channels.

Consistency in delivers and experience cements authority faster.

Enhance Visual Presentation

Elevating branding, layout and visual content enhances both visitor experience and professional optics.

Upgrade homepage design with clear calls to action for visitors to subscribe or purchase offerings. Maintain updated headshots and bios representing your expertise level credibly.

Ensure imagery and graphics make pieces more visually engaging while communicating more efficiently. Invest in original photos over stock imagery when feasible for authenticity.

Spend time reviewing competitive sites in your space as inspiration for visual improvements of your own that best align with brand identity.

Implement Paid Distribution

Once consistent in producing quality content, amplify reach through paid channels. Allocate annual budgets for paid social promotions on relevant pieces. Consider leveraging affiliate content networks like Taboola and OutBrain to insert related article recommendations across compatible websites.

Paid Newsletters sponsorships also expand subscriber totals overnight while positioning your expertise to new audiences. Capture wider viewership through strategic advertising for maximizing discovery beyond organic means alone.

Diversify Content Formats

Readers consume content today across far more than text-based blogs alone. Diversify creation into multiple formats to more deeply engage communities.

Alongside posts, produce slideshare Presentations unpacking research reports or industry trends. Create YouTube tutorial videos or vlogs documenting activities central to your niche. Launch weekly or monthly podcast interviews spotlighting unique industry perspectives.

Expanded content types showcase additional thought leadership facets more dynamically while giving current readers new ways to ingest your expertise.

Formalize Business Processes

Level up backend operations through formal systems supporting growth. Develop streamlined contributor guidelines enabling outsourcing creation for scaling output as audience expands.

Build rate cards and sales collateral for selling advertorial placements to sponsors consistently. Implement secure membership platforms facilitating insider community building through premium subscriptions.

With administrative components like analytics tracking and email sequence automation strengthened, focus shifts purely to quality content production moving forward.

Pursue Speaking and Media Opportunities

Elevated blogger positioning unlocks opportunities for offline influence and exposure.

Pitch appearances on relevant industry webcasts, fireside chats or podcast interviews. Seek quoting in mainstream media coverage of news relevant to your specialty. Develop complementary conference presentations or workshops around popular content themes. Position wider expertise through cross-channel visibility.

Proactive outreach for potential speaking, teaching and commentary amplifies impact beyond your blog itself. Become recognized as the informational ambassador around your distinct niche.

Next-Level Positioning

Implementing more sophisticated design, diversified content, paid distribution, operational foundations and offline visibility collectively takes your influence to the next level. Elevating perception and presentation builds loyalty with target readers while opening doors to profitable opportunities as the category-defining blog leader.

Conclusion

After covering numerous strategies for effectively monetizing blogs, boosting content production, expanding reach, and formalizing critical operations, how do you piece everything together for maximum success? While specifics will differ across niches and blogger goals, several fundamental best practices underpin lucrative and sustainable blogging ventures worth recapping.

Start with identifying your unique positioning and niche that guides content programming. Rather than general lifestyle musings, zero in on specialized knowledge and access most meaningful for a well-defined audience segment. Become known as the expert information hub around topics like sustainable living for families or training insights for marathon runners. Depth of value for a passionate community outweighs surface-level vanity metrics chasing wider casual audiences.

With niche cemented, implement diversified monetization combining multiple income streams -- from display ads to affiliate links to virtual events and coaching. Revenue diversity provides financial cushioning should any one channel underperform. More avenues also allow better matching monetization models to the natural interests of your community for non-intrusive user experience.

On operations, formalize business planning by treating your blog as a commercial media entity, not just a personal passion project. Build editorial calendars, hire support staff, secure legal protections, and track actionable analytics for growth. Specifically invest in high-quality visuals, user experience and content presentation to elevate legitimacy as your blog scales. Perception drives partnerships and sponsorship opportunities over time.

Regarding distribution, tap paid and earned channels for maximizing readership beyond organic search and shares alone. Sponsor social posts and newsletter ads on key content to efficiently expand reach to targeted groups elsewhere online. Proactively pitch relevant media commentary and industry events to further establish thought leadership offline as well.

And woven throughout all focus areas remains laser focus on consistently enriching user value. Survey audiences for product and content wishes. Monitor analytics for engagement patterns to double down on and refresh stale areas. Mentally filter all strategic decisions through the lens of "how does this benefit my loyal community" for continued win-win relationships driving viral growth.

Blogging at scale is far from simple, necessitating a diversity of creative, operational and technical competencies interfacing seamlessly. But the personal fulfillment and financial potential of building even a modest blog business centered on your unique passion makes the effort well worth it. With quality content as your compass, and sound business fundamentals propelling increased visibility and revenue channels, realize your thought leadership aspirations while turning your web presence into a flourishing commercial venture in the process.

Disclaimer

Though, every illustrated technique/secret in this book were aimed to show its readers the hidden way to making wealth, the author holds no responsibility to any consequence upon their applications by the readers.

Till we meet at the top, I wish you peace and riches.

….. Godwins Inkline.